T0067097

Ray of Hope

Ray of Hope

The Justo Lopez, Jr. Story

JUSTO LOPEZ JR.

authorHOUSE®

AuthorHouse™
1663 Liberty Drive
Bloomington, IN 47403
www.authorhouse.com
Phone: 1 (800) 839-8640

Published by AuthorHouse 04/10/2015

ISBN: 978-1-5049-0701-9 (sc)
ISBN: 978-1-5049-0700-2 (e)

Library of Congress Control Number: 2015905769

Print information available on the last page.

Any people depicted in stock imagery provided by Thinkstock are models, and such images are being used for illustrative purposes only.
Certain stock imagery © Thinkstock.

This book is printed on acid-free paper.

Chapter 1

Damn alarm, boy is it loud! I remember being mad cause I am not a morning person not at all. I wipe my eyes from that shit that film that is always around your eyes and eye lids. It's about 4 in the morning. I lean over from my side of the bed hoping not to wake evie up. I really don't want to wake her ass up. I didn't want to hear her shit so early in the morning because I woke her ass up. It's still dark outside. I lean over the side of the bed and my feet hit the warm rug because that's what we have, rug in our bedroom. I get to the bathroom, and turn on the light, still trying to be quiet. Well I wash my face and start doing the 3 things that all we guys do, shit, shave and shower. I look outside and boy is it still dark. I finish everything I had to do in the John.

I go downstairs after I am done and bring all my clothes I plan on wearing downstairs with me. I mean a lot of clothes. I go to wake up Keith and that boy was rocking the house he was snoring up a storm. I felt like giving him a wet Willie but I just couldn't. The night before he came over to hang out and we were playing spades. It is something we do every other Friday's night, or Saturday night back then. My friend Johnny boy, (that's what I call him.), called me and asked me if I wanted to go fishing on Saturday, which was the following day and I said hell yea. I love to go fishing!! He was going for strippers, and I have never caught a striper ever in my life so I was pumped. My eyes lit up. Johnny boy always told me how much fun the fight is against them type of fish, so I was very excited. Of course I had to ask my girlfriend at the time if I could go. She said in a very funny way, 'I am not your mom so do what you want!'... I laughed cause of the way she said it. I was going to go no matter what she said. She really didn't want me to go. I should have listened to her, now that I am telling the story. But when you wake up, u never know if it's your last day on earth. So u has to live every day like it's your last day in this life time.

So as the night got shorter, I asked Keith if he wanted to come with us. He said hell yea. So he went to his house so he could get some clothes because it was October and it was fucking cold out there. Beside I have gone out there in the ocean with Johnny boy before and it gets cold.

Well Keith comes back and we talk about the trip, not knowing the events coming up will change us for the rest of our lives, but we didn't know that yet. Well we went to sleep and as you can tell from the beginning of this page I was the 1st one up that morning. Well I come down the stairs and wake Keith up it was about 4:30 in the morning, we start getting dress, and boy did I get dress, you see it was October 15 2005 and it was cold that morning so me being a warm blooded Rican, I put so many pieces of clothing on me that couldn't believe it. I had 5 tee shirts, 2 long sleeves thermals on, and then I also put on 3 thermal pants and pajama pants also. I remember Keith laughing at me and he said, 'damn bro, Why so many clothes?' I laugh and said I am not a white boy papa, you people can take the cold but we Ricans need heat. We laugh and waited for Johnny boy. It was still dark as hell out there. Keith was saying," you Ricans are always late!' We started goofing on that....

Well Johnny boy shows up and we put all our stuff in his truck. You know the basics. We also took Jackets, cell phones, beer, lots of beer... that will be very important, not knowing that at that time that same beer would save my and the other guys lives.

Well we leave my apartment to go have fun fishing. We stop at a convenience store, they are everywhere were we live at on the East coast. While we were gassing up, we go inside to get some sandwiches for our trip. I was starving I really didn't eat the night before because I was excited for our trip. I got some Dramamine

2

so that way I won't get sea sick while were in the bay. I got some chips and other thing as you will read. I went to the register and paid for mine and Keith's stuff because I took all his loot the night before, I had to look out for him because that's how we roll in the shire. Keith is my brother. We met by fate. He was hanging with friends that we both know. We played dominoes and spades at a friend's home. We started talking and just hit it off. I took to him right away. I don't know why but I did. I could read people and he was a good person. My girlfriend at the time also took a liking to him. We spent a lot of time together. He will always be my BROTHER!!!!! Well there were a lot of people asking if we were going fishing, I was like hell yea we getting some stripers for dinner tonight. People were laughing saying you to funny Justo. You have to understand me I am a very friendly person that's my gift in life. I make people laugh in life. I am not the most handsome man in the world but, I am the most fun to be with. My wife Evelyn would say different. She thinks I am a so fucken fine. Well, I told one of the ladies that as they were making our sandwiches, if she hooked up our sandwiches we would bring her some fish and guess what! She did hook it us up very well. Damn, I owe her a fish…lmao I just remembered that.

So I leave the store and go help Johnny boy out with the gas and getting the fishing poles ready, so when we can get to where we're going. We don't have to do it there at the docks. We can just dock off and get to the bay and fish baby. So we start off down Delsea Drive. It was still dark at this time. We start talking about all the fish were going to fucking nail. This is the first time Keith comes out to fish with us and it might be his last! We start Listening to music and talking about who was going to get the biggest fish. Of course I was talking shit, cause hell that biggest fish will be mine. Johnny boy was saying in the truck that we had to be back by 2 because there was a party that he and his wife were going to. I also had a big birthday party to attend; my little sister Nellie was having a surprise party for her hubby's sister Susan Hewitt. My whole family was going to be there. When my sister Nellie has a party she always makes sure that I am there because, not to blast myself but I make shit happen so people like having me around. They just do.

3

Keith also had something to do that day, so that's why we wanted to be back at a good time. So we have 1 more stop, and that's for bait, but we couldn't find anything because the bait shops along the way were still close. We should have taken that as a sign. Well we get to Fortescue. I remember the wind was something awful. I remember it being so cold and windy. The sky was still cloudy. I was not feeling safe. You know that eerie feeling you get but can't explain why you feel that way, but i didn't say anything. Johnny boy goes and pays so we can dock off. Keith was in the truck fixing shit up. Making sure the food was in the boat.

I was in charge of getting the beer, so I had to put it away in these big ass coolers Johnny boy had, I mean you could put a body in there...lol later on in my story the coolers will come into play... In a Big way a big way!

Keith was crying about the wench because he had to crack it down so the boat can come off the trailer. While Johnny boy backed the truck into the water, the wind was blowing harder while they were doing that, I was on the boat still getting shit in order. We finally got the boat in the water, so we tide off on the dock while Johnny boy parked the truck and trailer in the parking lot. The wind was bad, I mean really bad. The water was choppy has hell the weather wasn't good.

By the time Johnny gets to the dock Keith is then done bitching about the cracking of the wench, he got the shit job. Since it was his 1st time with us he got stuck with the shit jobs, he just didn't know it. I was rolling from him bitching. His ears were red as red could be, I am telling you it was cold out there. But I guess that's the weather for stripers, so fuck it, let's go get those bitches. Whooppiieeeee

We had to stand on the dock, because there were other people there that got into the water before us. Its first come first gets in the water. So we started goofing around, cracking jokes and then we see our future but didn't know it. The water was really rough that day. As we were standing on the dock and checking out the

4

people that were there before us, getting ready to go out into the bay, there were these two black guys getting ready to go out into the bay, into those choppy, I mean really choppy water. I look at them guys and said. Them motherfuckers are crazy, they were in a fucking canoe, can u believe that Keith? Keith just nodded his head and Johnny boy said,' don't worry at least were in a boat', shit isn't going to happen to us out there. That sure wasn't going to be the truth people. And let's go on. I have a story to tell. I hope you like this ride, because it's a fucking while one. You will laugh, cry and live what I lived, on Oct.15, 2005. Let's take a ride. You guys ready. Get some tissues.

Chapter 2

As our journey begins, we finally get our turn to leave the dock, at that point the water wasn't that bad and since Johnny boy's boat was a nice size I felt safe. Johnny boy said were going to the sticks that are a spot in the bay that people go fishing for strippers. It's like 6 miles into the bay. The ride was choppy as we headed into our fate. Not knowing what was going to happen on this life changing day.

I was so glad that I took my sea sick pills and so did Keith. Johnny boy never took any cause he thought he was the man, later on he will regret that move.

While were going deeper into the waters, the wind was picking up again and we stop to see where we were at. We sat there for a little bit and just checkout the bay. It was still a gloomy day and still cold and windy. I was cold and warm at the same time. I guess because I was scared and happy at the same time. I have always loved to fish but really never went until I met Johnny boy. He has taken me to so many spots. to go fishing in the past.

I remember one day he took me down the river in Millville New Jersey, that's the next town from where we live. Anyway, we caught a lot of little fish but we had a good time doing just that Fishing. Since then, Johnny boy and I always went out together fishing when we could. We went down the river in Millville all the time. But that was for catfish and other little fish. Today we were going for big fish baby strippers.

While we were sitting there, Johnny boy was making sure everything was ok on the boat. He checked everything. Life vests, lights, the horn, we had a fish finder machine and some other kind of g.p.s thing. And then this mother fucker comes out with a map that we couldn't read...lol we weren't captain of fishing! We were 3 guys going fishing for fun. So I didn't know how to read those types of maps. The only thing that wasn't working was the radio. The c.b radio.

Keith was busy eating his breakfast, we made his ass work, well I did, I figured I bought him, and I took all his money playing spades the night before. But later on he saved me from bugging out. You will understand what I mean later in my side of the story. So I go and join Keith and have a little bit of my breakfast, while Johnny boy was busy doing his thing on the boat. Johnny boy didn't want to eat. It was still windy and the water was getting a little rough. But we decided to ride it out a little. So we just talked about random shit you know, I started talking about my 1st grandson juju. I was talking about him playing baseball and all the wonderful things a 1st time grandpa talk about. You know things you didn't get to do with your kids; I was going to make sure I did them with my grandson Derek. Then we talked guy shit, like are you banging the old lady good, how many blow jobs this you get this week, men talk. Poor Keith didn't have a girl back then. So he couldn't talk about a good blow jobs or any other sex shit guys talk about. lol

So we decide to go, so we go out to the sticks that are what they're called. That was our spot to hit. I was just sitting there while we took our 6 mile run into the bay, on the ride of our lives. U could see all kind of stuff. I see a light house, giant ass oil tankers, boy they look so fucking far away. I remember looking at them and thinking they must be so fucken big cause I can see them from here so imaged how big they are in person. That was cool to see. While we were riding up there towards the sticks all I remember from where we docked off was the top of roof houses and then tree top, you could barely see the tops of both of them. The trees and tops of houses, the A frame of houses.

I remember I didn't see know birds at all, I thought that was strange, cause you always see some kinds of birds out there. It must have been about 8 in the morning when we got to this one spot. So we let the anchor out and started fishing. Let's see what happens here. The water was still choppy but not that bad, like before so we were happy about that. The sun was peaking threw. It was trying to break thru the clouds. We stood at this spot. It looked good and then the sun was starting to really come out. It was like we were meant to have a great day of fishing. It was crazy. The suns reflection was bouncing off the water like it was glass. It looked like glass or like a mirror. It really looked beautiful. It was so peaceful.

Then all the sudden we start catching fish galore. I mean we were killing them. We had two coolers like I said earlier. One full of beer with ice, and the other one were for the fish. There were about 4 boats were we were at. I remember a big ass party boat around us. All of a sudden the water started to get calm and the sun finally came out full force out, so the day started getting better. We decided to move to another spot that Johnny boy knew. You see he has been out here numerous times and he knew the area well. So we moved on.

I had called my girlfriend when we got too our next stop. Just wanted to let her know that we were ok and we were getting some fish. She asked me if we were still going to Susan's party at my sister's Nellie's house later that evening and I told her but of course baby, you know there is no party without this Rican. She was rolling with laughter. Going back in time, I remember the first time I met Evelyn.

Chapter 3

When I first met Evelyn, we met online. I had a profile on the internet and she had seen it. She took the chance when I wrote that some people say I look like. Richard Pryor. She thought that would be cool to have someone who is happy all the time. So she and hit me up. She told her sister that she met a man and he looks just like Prince. Evelyn is a huge Prince fan from way back in the day. She was all R&B and I loved my guitar music. Kiss was my favorite group back then but I will tell u more about that later as my story goes. Well, she was divorced after a bad marriage and it was just her and her son Eric. She would call him My Eric and I thought she would be good woman to have around. The fact that we both went thru bad divorces, made it easy for her and I to understand relationships and what our expectation are and what shit we would not put up with. Perfect. I never wanted to get married again anyways. That is a pain that never would wish on anyone. It really effects the kids in a bad why... So, Evelyn and I decided to meet one day. We spoke to each other a few weeks before deciding to hook up. After all, I have had my share of wild rides and I wasn't trying to go that route this time. She drove down from up north on a Saturday evening. Whoopieeeeeee!!!

Well, we met at a public spot cause that's the right thing to do. She could have been a serial killer I didn't know. LOL We met at a Wawa parking lot. I was sitting there waiting on her and she pulls up. When lightening hits you, it is for sure an ass kicker. She smiled at me and I was hook. But I had to play it cool. I am Justo. We chat a few moments and I wanted her to meet my parents. I knew off the bat she was different and I caught her eyeing me

9

up a few times too. (Wink) At that time I was living with my folks. We entered the my house and Evelyn brought this cinnamon loaf bread for my parents. I was not aware she was going to do this. I figure this was her style and she did appeared to be generous and kind. My dad said, 'this is the one! You need to keep her Justo. You better keep her.' You have to understand something about me; I was single and willing to mingle. My mom was always mad at me because I had all these different women coming over and picking me up. My dad on the other hand would just look at me never saying anything! All he did was shake his head. I never forgot that. So when he told me to keep her I took a chance. Evelyn and I started a relationship. We spend time together every weekend and fell in love. At that time I didn't know she was going to save my life one day.

So after that we started making plans for her to move out here to Vineland New Jersey. She took a chance and came down and found a job at the local hospital. We found an apartment and moved in together. Everything was great; we had little fights here and there but nothing big. One day I remember she brought up the subject of marriage and I told her, don't ever bring that shit up. I mean I did it once and got really hurt. I never wanted to be hurt like that again... Never. One day Evelyn had said to me....what is wrong; am I not good enough to marry? That stuck in my head.

She did not bring it up again.

Later on, in my story you will understand why I mention this part of my life with Evelyn.

Justo and Evelyn at an event

Chapter 4

So we left the spot we were in and moved to another area searching for fish. I look around and all I saw was water. It was everywhere. The calm waters became very choppy and it rocked the boat like a mother would be rocking a crying baby.

I wasn't feeling right so I went down the bottom cabinet to lay down for a bit. I closed my eyes for about 40 minutes just lost in my own thoughts. I could not relax. I was trying to understand why I felt so uneasy on this trip out. I had hoped it would pass so I could join my brother's topside. I got up feeling better than I did earlier. The sun was out and the bay water was like a piece of glass. It was so, so still. Calm.

The sky had A few clouds but it was blue as I remember it looking at our last trip in Florida we took to get away and relax. Evelyn and I did some traveling back in the day. Her motto was, have car will travel. She would get up on a Saturday, cook me breakfast and we would just drive. Where we landed did not matter. It was fun singing our favorite songs as I would touch her in places where she would have to say, stop it! But I knew she likes the attention. Yep, the sky looked great and the water was clam.

Meanwhile getting back to the story. Keith and Johnny boy were catching fish, a lot of fish. I got something to eat. I had a couple of beers and then started fishing myself. We started talking about life and that's when I decided that I would ask Evelyn to marry me. I didn't say anything to the guys yet.

There were a couple of other boats around us. I remember there was a big green party boat about 100 yards from us. Then to the far right there was a blue and white speed boat about 300 yards away.

So I felt safe, you have to remember that were 6 miles into the bay.

Things were going good until the water started its shit again. It got choppy. The boat was being tossed from one wave to only have another hit us. The water started to move fast and we were rocking faster. It was hard to walk from one end to another. We started taking on water but again we thought the pump was on but never once thought it wasn't. So the party boat left our area. The only other boat was that blue and white one. The water became calm again. We chatted again for a while; it was around 11:50 then. Johnny boy and I were on the side of the boat and I think Keith was in the front of the boat doing his thing. The sky started to cloud up and it started to get colder. At that moment I started talking to Johnny boy about real life shit. I had to tell someone my plans about asking Evelyn to marry me.

I said to Johnny boy, "the next big party that's going to happen is mine papa". He was like what are u talking about Justo? I said, we need a bachelor party papi! I said to Johnny boy, It's been a while since we had a blowout party; I am going to ask Evelyn to marry me. He couldn't believe me. All that shit you said about marriage Justo, how you would never do it again, what happen? I told him about what Evelyn told me that day about not being good enough to marry. And how it never ever left my mind and I knew that she was the one for me. He was so happy for me and her. He asked when I was going to pop the question.

On her birthday which is a month away on Nov, 11, 2005. Johnny boy gives me a big ass hug, and said you're a lucky man because Evelyn is the greatest; she always takes care of you and all of us also. She also loves your friends. Good job Justo. I was happy inside. It had been a long time I felt this happy. I mean so happy that nothing in the world could make you feel anything less. I took the plunge. I made up my mind. Next month I will ask her

13

to be my wife. My family will unite and we will all be as one again. If only my daughter Jessy would allow me to be in her life again. Marrying Evelyn will help heal the old wounds. Shit, I feel better already! We will have a church wedding. I did not have that in my first marriage. I will do it right. I stood up from my thoughts as I felt the boat rocking faster and the waves seem angry. Lord, are you mad at me? What did I do wrong? I only want to make things right with Evelyn and me!

Within 15 minutes the sky was getting gloomy dark clouds, and I was thinking, what the fuck. Then it began. The waves were hitting so very hard on the boat that it shook the boat like a twig in a wind storm. As the waves were coming over the front and back of the boat, water was spraying large droplets as it was smacking us around. It made me think if it was thunder storming too?

The sea seemed to be getting mad at that time. The swells of water were at least 4 to 5 feet high. The boat started to take on water from the back end. Keith was at the front of the boat, and I can see the waves were hitting him hard. I remember we were looking at each other as to say is this shit really fucking happening? I see his eyes and they told me that we were in serious danger. Johnny boy started screaming at me to cut the anchor, cut the anchor! I was standing there looking at the water as it was flowing into the boat, trying to get the knife but there was all kind of shit floating all over the place. Water is now over my knees. My knees! I started to get the knife that was floating all over the deck. Water was everywhere. It was hard to find anything because of all the waves hitting the boat. I mean they were coming from everywhere. One wave finally got me. I was in shock at that moment. Then another wave fucking knocked me to the floor. Johnny boy was still trying to start the engine. The engine wasn't turning over! I can hear him trying to turn the engine over but it was stalling out. Meanwhile, I saw Keith jumped into the water to try to pull the rope with the anchor out from the bottom. The water was all over! It surrounding me and it was now trying to take us off the only solid surface we were now partially swimming in. Stuff was floating all over and my mind was racing. I couldn't believe what was happening. One minute I am telling

Johnny Boy that I am getting married and then next the boat is starting to sink. Keith starts to come back onto the boat from the water. He couldn't get the anchor out from the bottom. Johnny Boy starts yelling at me. The life vests Justo, get the life vests, and get the vests! I got up from the floor to make my way towards the compartment where the vests were at. As I get to the area where the vest were at another wave hit the boat and the vessel started to sink from the back end. Johnny boy was still trying to start the boat. The boat started to sink very fast from the back, that the front was rising up!! What a sight! The waves were hitting me and Johnny boy. Let me tell you, the force of water is no joke. It took all I could muster to open the cabinet where the life vests were in. Johnny boy was yelling to get the vests, get the vests as he was running in knee high water towards me. With the will of God while the water was crashing on top of us, I was finally able to get the compartment door open. Johnny boy was able to reach in while I held open the doors and he pulled three life vests out and threw them into the water as the boat took on more water. Johnny boy jumped into the water and I was right behind him. Keith was the last one to jump out of the boat.

I hit the water like an Olympic driver. I had so many pieces of clothing on that I was sinking to the bottom of the bay fast. I scramble to grab a vest and held on to it for dear life. I was in shock! I couldn't believe that I am out in the bay! No more solid footing. I am in the freaking deep blue bay next to the Atlantic Ocean. We set out to have a great time doing something we all love and now shit. How did it come to this? The water was freezing! The water was choppy and the sky went from sky blue to darkness. God, what are you doing today too us?

My thoughts were racing in my mind as the water was taking me into its mouth. Again I asked myself why me, not like this God.

The sun was blinding as it reflected off the water. We looked at the boat and it was the craziest thing you would ever witness. The boat raised up from the front as the back of the boat sank. The front of the boat looked like it was sitting on its ass while the nose was pointing up towards the sky. It was crazy. We go towards the boat and all sudden the front of the boat started to rise higher in the air, I mean it looked like crazy shit, it looked like the titanic was sinking. The back of the boat is totally under water. No joke! Just like in the movies but this was real life action in front of us. In less than ten sec, the boat sank!!! It was the most exciting and terrifying thing I have ever witness. The way the bay took that boat as if it was hungry. The bay wanted to be fed with the dam boat we were just on. And then there was no boat. No fucking boat. I saw Keith finally grabbing a life vest as he lay on top of it. Johnny boy was putting his jacket on in the water and we all just look at each other. In complete silence. I don't know what was going through their minds, but my mind was going crazy. I could not focus on one single complete thought. My heart was pounding so fast it felt it was in my throat trying to escape this hell we were in. Once there was a boat, fish, plenty of beer, laughter and now nothing. How did this happen? Why?

I was just on a boat one moment confessing to one of my best friends how I am in love with this woman, and how I am going to ask her to marry me and 15 minutes later, the fucking boat sank. I saw what is going on but I couldn't keep a straight thought. I saw two of my friends in the water and it was trying to sink them. We started to talk to each other. Keith came towards me and I am trying to make sense of this ordeal were in, and what can we do. Keith starts yelling, 'Justo, Justo,' with authority because it was hard to hear anything. The wind was howling and the waves are crashing on us. It was cold. God, I can' think. God, why is this happening?

Chapter 5

So, at the apartment, Evelyn tried calling Justo again as 12 o'clock in the afternoon is rolling around. It has been many hours since she last heard from him. This was not like him not to call and 'check in' to make sure all was well at home and just to say hello. She is becoming worried but not sure why she is feeling worried. She wonders if something is wrong and begins to pace around the apartment looking for something to do to keep her mind focus. He was due back soon as they had to attend a birthday party later that evening. The family were all going to be at the party and Justo enjoys being around people and this wasn't like him not to call. She decides to wash the dirty clothes and this will take up a few hours to put away that 'feeling' that we get when we know something is wrong. She should have trusted her feelings.

Chapter 6

I looked at Keith and I could see the look of fear in his eyes. I saw the blue in his eyes and they were as big as saucers. The dark spot of his eyes were gone. I can laugh about at that now, because I know I had that same look too. He starts telling me what to do. First, he tells me, 'I am coming towards you Justo, don't panic ok?' 'Look at me Justo! Look at me!' He says in a commanding voice. I shake my head to say yes. He starts to tell me he was a life guard before and for me not to panic. He then says, 'don't try and hit me, I am coming to help you with your vest.' I knew what to do but as I was in shock I needed to realize what was happening at that moment. He tells me take off my boots and all of my clothes. I knew what he was saying was true but I needed to hear that from him. He says, you're going to be weigh down, he kept saying as he is looking at me, 'look at me Justo: everything is going to be ok brother, come on brother come on!! I knew what I had to do. I took of my Timberland boots and let them sink to the bottom of the bay. They will never be seen again. Keith is coming closer towards me, and he kept saying,' Justo I am going to help u with your life vest because I was only holding on to it. It wasn't around me. I had a death grip and I wasn't letting go.

He proceeded to help me by just talking to me. The sound of his voice made me come back to reality. There goes another wave all in our faces. The bay was still mad as it continued to be choppy. Johnny boy was in shock as he bobbed in the water. I didn't see him for about 5 min. I am still taking off all of my clothes, because I didn't want them to sink me and the waves weren't helping either. I finally got all my clothes off, but now I was naked. Butt naked. The water was cold against my skin. I remember keeping just my nose and eye's above water because, the sun was bright again. You're not going to believe this but I thought I was in a dream. This can't be real. And there goes another wave up side my face. It brings me back to the place I don't want to be. Keith then proceeded to help me with my vest. And guess what, I was ass out cause it was a vest for a kid, yea I said a kid, if it wasn't rough enough, we were in the bay with a boat that sunk and I got a fucking kids life vest. Can you believe it!! It wouldn't click together, and it wouldn't zipper up, what the fuck. So I said to myself, 'I am assed out'. Ok how can we make something work? Keith was still next to me. Shit the water is cold! We got together for a brief time in the water. I pictured myself dying. My first thought ever of actually dying. I will be gone from Evelyn, my daughters, my parents and my first grandson. This can't be happening to me!! Not me! Not me! I do remember the looks I seen in Johnny boy and Keith faces. Terror. I never used that word before to describe anything in my life other than this moment. I knew I must have had the same look. Terror.

We were into about 15 mins. into this crazy ass shit, with the Sun out now, and it was starting to get really bright at this time. The water became calm again. So Keith said, 'what are we going to do?' 'What are we going to do?' Mean while he was looking at me while he is saying this. I look at myself with one hand holding my vest closed and the other trying to swim while treading water and fucking butt naked. I start to look around and notice the very, very tops of roofs and a lot of tree tops also in the far distant of some type of land. About 2 miles that way maybe?

I remember them also, what I mean is that I remember the tree tops from fishing earlier. Johnny boy was saying while we were riding into the sticks that's the place we were heading to start fishing at. To get back to the docks, we had to follow the top of the roof from them house's. So that stuck in my head. So I remember that at that moment. Keith said, 'Justo what do we do?' Johnny boy said we have to get to land. Land that is 2 miles away with me holding my life vest closed and trying to swim with one arm? Do they think I am capable of doing this? I doubted myself and our awful situation. What the fuck!

Anyway, the water was calming down now, and Keith was still by my side. I looked at him in a way that I have never looked at anyone in my life. I told him he had to go get help. Johnnyboy started to swim towards the top of the trees and that's the last time I saw him. I wasn't sure if I was ever going to see him again. Would we ever have other fishing trips? Nah, fuck that! I will never fish in salt water again. But I hoped Keith wouldn't leave but he had to get help. He was the only one thinking straight in this hell at this moment.

Keith is crying and telling me he isn't leaving me. I told him to look at me!! Look at me. I have one hand that has to hold up my life vest! (All the sudden the water went clam really flat.) In the distance, I saw Johnny boy swimming towards the trees. God I hope he finds help for us all. There was a look of terror in Keith eye's so I tell him everything's going to be aright papa. You guys are my only hope papi. He was saying please Justo please come follow us. But I couldn't, I couldn't swim. The life vest doesn't fit. I started crying because I knew I would never see him or Johnny again. Get the fuck out of here and get fucking help!! Get out!!!!!!!..................

Chapter 7

Now Evelyn is getting down right mad that it has been almost 9 hours since I left to go fishing. She is clock watching but her instincts are telling her something that she cannot make the piece of the puzzle fit. She called more times than she ever would before. Evelyn is not one to hound me when I leave the house. She gives me my space that allows me to be me. I would not ever do anything to break that trust or hurt her. A woman as Evelyn does not come too often. I screwed up my first marriage for many dumb reasons but this second chance was going to have my full attention. Evelyn is putting away the clothes she washed and now all she has on her hands is time. But five minutes seem endless to a woman who is watching the clock. I hope she knows how much I wish I could be there to help ease her fears. Man, I hope she isn't thinking anything stupid as I want to only be there with her now.

Chapter 8

He look one last time at me and He said,' I love you man, I love you', I was saying the same thing to him also, that I loved him. I was screaming to him to tell Evelyn that I love her with everything I have. She has changed my life. I love her tell her!! As he was leaving, he said shit I should have stayed home today, at that moment, I felt like it was my fault that he was out there with his life in my hands and I let him down. It didn't start off like that this and now here we are, fucking fighting for our lives. If I survive this and he doesn't how could I look at his mother and brother what would I say? Would they forgive me? I told him to keep screaming so I could hear his voice so that way we could at least hear each other. But as time went by, the sounds where getting farther and farther apart. Until all I heard were the waves and the wind. I realize I am on my own. Shit what to do, what I do.

I no longer hear Keith, and the waves are getting bad, for every two or three strokes I took the waves threw me back 5 feet, so to guess. I am holding my vest with one hand and trying to swim with the other, what a mess am I in. how would in my wildest thoughts, would I be in this predicament. Keithhhhh at the top of my lungs I yell, with whatever I had in me, and nothing! Silence.

And then a funny thing hit me, I saw the top of house's. There was hope. There was hope. I have a friend a best friend. His name is Richard Rivera Sr. and he is an army man, G.I Joe shit and he always told me when we were playing handball and we were down, to dig in deep and look into yourself and let's get over the hump Justo, come on. And we did win a lot of games lol....

So there I was, with a big game to play and the stakes are life and death. What to do? I choose to fight and fight I did, till the death baby, till the death.

I started to remember that white and blue boat that was speeding off while we were trying to walk on water, yelling help us, help us. As it took off I realized it never even seen us damn, damn.

The water was calming down at this time. The sun was getting brighter and the water was a little warmer also. I was still in disarray because I am stuck in the bay. I start to look around and this time I am making sense of what's going on. I have thoughts in my mind that real life is in front of me.

Ok let's fight. I keep my nose and eye's above water because the waves are not bad at this moment. Holy shit I see a giant oil tanker, damn it looked like it was at the edge of the world. Now I had something to focus on, something to really see. I got more hope, more hope.

It must have been about 2 in the afternoon. The sun was bright and it was warm. The water was warm also. Well for me it was. by now, I kept looking up to the sky cause that's how I was trying to tell time, I don't know how I know that but I do. So I go towards the tanker. I tread water with my legs and with one hand start to swim towards the tanker, the water is flat so I have a chance, I figured if they see my vest or at least see something in the water they would stop, Wishful thinking at that time. I continue onward I was feeling good about getting close towards it, but it was a very long, long ways away. But there was hope.

As I am making my way there towards the tanker here come the fucking waves, I couldn't believe it not again, just then hope is in my favor, there it goes. Shit, shit, shit....

The waves were taking me down now under the water. The waves were no fucking lie, about 10 to 15 feet high and then when they curled they were landing on me and taking me down into the bay at one point I hit the bottom of the bay floor.... At one moment, my vest came completely off. It was about 5 feet away from me. I kept swimming to get my life vest back. That was a trip. At that moment if I didn't get that jacket back I was dead. And I am not giving up, not yet anyways. I finally get it back and start putting it on.

Thanks to God that I ate all that food on the boat cause I had enough energy for ten people that day baby. But that shitty life vest! Why me with this one. Good thing Junie didn't come with us. He wanted to come but when johnnyboy called him in the morning the bitch didn't fucken get up. If he did I don't know if I would be telling you guys about this story. There would have been 4 of us and three vests, what a war that would have been... They kept hitting me, the waves were. But they weren't as bad as the last 10 mins. I started to think about my life at that time. How I just found a beautiful woman who loves me more than anything in the world. A life that was making me very happy. I went through a divorce and have 2 daughters, my oldest girl Jessica didn't talk to me anymore during the break up and my youngest girl Julie did. Jessica and I were very close as were Julie and I. But Jess was the tomboy and Julie was the hair and nails stuff. I used to have tea parties and let them paint my nails and toes, shit that's what daddies do for their girls. That thought came to my head, happy times. I felt warm. It made me cry. I have to see my girls again, tell them how much they mean to me, how much I love them, how I need them IN my life. I always looked for them.

Jessy use to play baseball. She was the only girl In Scalfo history who played for an all boy team. She was nasty. She had natural talent. I use to throw bottle caps which we use to call chap-pas (Spanish) and she would knock them out of sight. She was my first. How I love my daughter. The first time I looked into her eyes I knew I was a sucker for real love. She was of my blood. My gene pool. I love this person. I want to be able to tell her this. She had to know how much love I have for her, always.

Julie was the girly girl of the two but she stuck by me after the divorce. She knew I love her but I needed to hold her again. I needed to tell her how she was still my babygirl. She gave me my first grandson. My first boy. My juju. Good luck. I could use some good juju now. I was remembering taking Julie out every Tuesday to get her nails done or just to go eat. Spending time with her. She is my baby. Jessy is my oldest but Julie is my baby. So they both hold a piece of my heart. Evelyn holds the rest. Will I ever see my beautiful girls again? I thought of my mother. She took us out of a hell whole and gave us a great life. She did the best she could for me and my sister Marisol, Angel, Nellie, and Armando. Mommy, mommy... I start to cry.....

That's the kind of shit that was running threw my head at that time. Shit there goes another wave and here I go again trying to fight the waves. Then I see sticks that are where we were heading to begin with. They looked like there were about 200 yards away. I go towards them; I go under the water again. The waves kept hitting me and taking me under again. I come up gasping for air. I sallow some of the bay water again and boy was it salty. I know I can't really drink it because it will really dehydrate you.

I see shark fins and think what should I do? If I make too much splashing sounds will the sharks get me? I lay on my back at that moment. I was scared shit less. The last thing and the worsted thing to think about is a shark. A fucking shark. What the hell am I going to do? We seen some sharks earlier but we were on a boat then. It's a lot different when the sharks are swimming all around you. I never felt so all alone in my life. Another bump in this, adventure called life. And right now it's my life were talking about.

Chapter 9

I lay there on top of the water crying, is this for real; God is this the way it ends for me? I am so happy right now. My life is getting better. I can't die like this, not like this. I start to get a little crazy cause, first of all I am in the fucken bay and there are sharks at my feet, my vest doesn't fit, and I am cold. I punch myself in the face so I could wake up. I was getting tried, much tried. I let the waves take me and I float away with the waves. I start to think about johnnyboy and Keith how are they doing? Did they get back together? Are they safe? are they getting me help? I start to think about my grandson again. The 1st one I have. My juju. I call him that cause I believe in, if you help someone in need, you do it with love, and please pay it forward. That's good juju. So that's why I gave him that name. He only lets me call him juju. If you call him by the name I gave him he will let you know Only papa Justo call's me by that name. He came to my mind. I think back too, when my little girl Julie told me she was with child. It hit me, damn a grandkid. How was it going to be? And he is a boy. I mean it was a blessing, because I helped raised two girls and you know a father always wants a boy so he could give him everything you never had. I feel in love with him without even meeting him yet. Well we didn't know if it was a boy or girl, but a grandkid. Shit the waves just took me under again. What am I going to fucking do? I remember how peg called me and said Julie is in labor, and that was at about 1 in the morning March, 31, 2005. Evelyn stood home and allowed me to enjoy this moment when that phone call came. 9 long months waiting for him. Mu Juju. I get there to the hospital, and I head towards the labor room. I was chilling with my ex-wife Peggy and my oldest daughter Jessica, and were waiting for our new addition, to our family. Boy was he a sight. Like the song by creed (with eyes wide open). His eyes were so damn big and brown. He was Looking everywhere at that moment. I fell so in love with him, like I did with my 2 daughters. Those memories kept me fighting. I thought, damn am I getting to see him grow up? Will I teach him how to play baseball, football? Teach him how to be a man? That people will respect. All the things I wish I would have had. Not a person who talks at you. But a person shows you how to be a man. And someone you could talk too, not someone talking at you. Some people can understand what I am talking about. I hope.

Evelyn is getting our clothes ready for the family birthday party. She has hope I will be there to go with her to see the family and hang out for the evening. She has hope. She is mad but that is okay. She has hope and faith in me. But man, she is not too happy that I have not called. But I think she is more concern than truly mad. She knows this isn't my routine with us. I call this woman all the time just to say, "I love you," and just to hear her smile on the other end. She looks for this. It makes her heart sing and it makes life brighter for us both. We are both dealing with second changes. This keeps us honest and real. If she only knew how much I wanted to be there at home.

So here I am in the middle of the bay, with water crashing all around me. I get my bearings kind of straight buy now. I see some sticks in the bay so I head towards them. I laugh and say there is hope, so I hold my vest like I have been holding it. With one hand holding my vest together and trying to swim I went towards the sticks. But for every stroke I took, I kept getting thrown back 5 feet and the waves were sinking me again.

So I decided to go through the waves, fuck it, if I could still crash threw the middle of the waves while they were at their peak I could make it to the sticks. So I did that for about an hour. I road waves, rain, cause of the way the waves crashes against the water. Waves those were so high that when you walk the streets in Manhattan, you look straight up. Everything was still splashing all around me, god what am I going to do, what am I am going to do.

Every time I have something good and going my way, the sea said no way, you're not going to make it. But I had other plans baby. I am not just giving up that easy. so that's why I kept fighting for life. I started to think again of the guys. Where are they? Are they ok? No more Keith and I yelling to each other. I start to cry again. Why now god why now. I look up and say to the sky, looking thru the clouds searching for god himself. Wishing God was looking at me at that moment, just looking at me, not at no one else.

I told my God, please let me live though this as I was thinking about my mother. She has been so happy that I have found a woman that she loves. I wanted to make my mom proud of me for just once in my life. Just one dam time.

As for the rest of my family, my sisters and brothers they ran thru my mine as well as my dad, he was the one who told me to keep Evelyn. Another wave hits me… I almost lost my vest with that dam wave. I guess I got caught in a rip, because it felt like three hits at once.

I started to say my last rite's, telling god that I was so sorry for the bad things I have done in my life, I wasn't the best kid or young man growing up, I should have been a better person as I was thinking as my life flashed by me. I have done bad things to other people and felt like if I only had another chance I could be a better person. I went back in my memory of New York where my mom went to beauty school to take care of me, Marisol and Angel. Mom had it tough. Where did she get the strength to be a good mom for us? I found the strength as I reached out my arms and floated on my back as peace came over me. I had closed my eyes to confess my sins. My family was my last single thought. I was saying goodbye to everyone as God watch me. My girls, my girlfriend, my mom, my first grandson Keith and Johnnyboy please remember how much I love you.

Then the water was flat. It was at peace. The water gave me the signal it was time. Now is the best time. I gave up. I took my last breathe. I let the vest go from around me and started to sink to the bottom. I look up while I am sinking; my vest is still in my

28

hand while I felt the bottom of the bay calling me. Then All of a sudden the funking vest was at my side like it was taking me back up to the water. I start to swim back up to the top of the water. I was gasping for air and my vest is still there. I can't believe that all this is happening to me. I know longer see any sticks, or the top of trees or tops of houses. What is it u want from me God?

As I came to the top of the water I laid on my back and looked up to the sky and just started to say the prayer of the lord. The water was flat at that moment. All of a sudden a wave took me and tosses about 30 feet I was in the air for a minute as if it was effortless and there it was. A pole in the middle of this water! Where the hell did it spring from? How far was I tossed by that one wave? How was the pole being supported? There it was. A metal pole was sticking out of the middle of the bay. A metal fucken pole! I blinked several times to make sure it was what I was truly seeing. My eyes light up like it was the night sky of the fourth of July. No way, I can't believe what I see, it can't be for real, I was thinking here goes hope again. I start swimming my way towards the pole with everything I have in me. I had to swim with one hand holding my vest cause it didn't fit. My other hand was going towards that pole. I start to smile because I am saying to myself if I make it to that pole, I could hold on till help gets here. I can live, see my girls and my girlfriend and the rest of my family, and we all can joke about another crazy thing that happens to Justo.

I get to that pole and love it like a man loves a woman. It was my life line, my way back home. You have to understand that in that place in time all I had was that pole. The bay was getting bad as I held on to the pole, which I am still in aww of how it got to me. Is god really letting me live, or does he have a plan for me. The waves were softening up on me. I had my hand on my vest holding it together and my other hand holding the pole while fighting the waves. You couldn't image what it was like.

Fighting the bay waters and trying to hold on to a wet slimy pole was a mother humpier. I started to really cry with joy and sorrow because all of different kind of great memories was going through my mind. My family. We had many great Christmas when I was married to Peggy. The family was all life was about back then. My girls were the first grandchildren and nieces on my side. They were spoiled everyday and with every chance someone in the family could provide. Jessie had to have this ventriloquist doll. She loved that thing. Julie with her hair/nail girly stuff that she loved to have and do daily. The family gave to the kids always and they never needed anything. My family. I have to get my mind straight and focus on the task at hand, my life. I wanted to see them with their children in our future.

Justo with daughters and grandsons

I see big giant tankers in the horizon, thinking if they come my way, I am dead. There is no way they would see me and they would run my ass over and no one will know otherwise. No way. Well I kept looking up at the sky to try to tell time. From my guess at that moment it was about 3-4 in the afternoon, three to maybe 5 hours after our boat sank. I was holding the metal pole that was sticking out of the bay; it had to be at least 50 feet high. You have to remember we were fishing in the bay so that water is deep already. When we were fishing johnnyboy had the sonar on it was reading 17 to 30 in depth, so when I got to that pole, it was at least 20 high, from the top of the water to the sky. It was a stairway to heaven. Peace. Safety?

I couldn't believe I got to that pole was what I thought as I was hugging it with a death grip. I was feeling the heat of the sun on my back. It was a good feeling. I needed heat. The water was cool and I was feeling it. The sun was such a blessing.

The bay was clam for now, and I just started to think about my life again. If I live what will I do, to become a humble and better person. What will I do with a second chance at life? I was thinking about Keith and Johnny boy. Where are they? Did the make it to shore and are they getting me help. I started too slip up and down the pole from the waves coming over top of me. I held on for dear life people. It felt the bay was playing a game with me. First it was calms one moment then the next thing the waters and waves got out of hand. At one point I was fighting 30 feet waves. Waves that was as high as city skyscrapers. The waves felt as if they were cement buildings crashing on and around me. I know it hard to believe for some people. You have no idea what the water can do when it wants too. It has emotion. It is very temperamental. It is controlling.

At one point, the waves forced me down to the bottom of the bay. I was holding on the metal pole as the waves took me down. I was starting again to give up on life because what the fuck else am I going to go thru.

I stayed under the water for heat and on the bottom of the pole the small clams were cut the shit out of my feet. I had to hold my foot up so the blood won't go into the bay. I was worrying now about sharks. They can smell blood 3 miles away. Cold water, rolling waves, potential sharks. What the hell else and I to force to deal with. What did I do in my life that was so bad that I was going thru this ordeal?

Chapter 10

All kind of shit was running thru my mind. I just wanted to go to sleep. Just a little nap that's all I needed, thinking to myself. But all of all a sudden I started to fights with me. We were having a conversation. It wasn't me, myself, and I. it was just me and myself this time. I started to hit myself in the in the face so I could continue to fight with this mess I got myself into. I wanted to see my new born grandson grow up. I wanted to help my daughter teach him to become a respectable man that people look up to. I wanted to be that man too. I needed to erase my past life of pain and build a better tomorrow. I wanted to marry my girlfriend. I just started a great new life. Things were finally going good for me. I had a great job. So I kept fighting for my life, fuck it I am going to fight to the end that's my plight.

So here I am fighting the weather because it was getting colder out. Then the wind was also picking up. The sun was going down so I figure it's about 3- 4 pm in the afternoon, remember the time moved forward an hour. Well that's what I remember. Daylight savings time.

Evelyn is home dressed up for the party. I know she looks beautiful and her eyes are made up and I love how the gold shines in her brown eyes when she smiles. She is pacing the floor. She wants to call someone just to know that I am okay and for some crazy reason, I just have not called. I couldn't call. My phone is on the ocean floor! She is now talking to herself trying to choose the best way to call someone without triggering fear or risk sounding jealous asking about me. She chooses not to call anyone as to keep hope and trust between us. If she only knew how much I wanted to be there. She is getting scared.

At one point, I really hit myself really hard that I was bleeding from my nose. I was feeling myself getting sleepy. I needed to wake up and hang on to this pole that was bouncing with the waves with me on it. I felt like a cowboy in a rodeo. The blood wasn't flowing that bad from my nose. It was Just enough for me to taste it on my lips. So I get to the top of the poll and fix myself up to where I can be one with the pole. I was a mess. My mind was thinking about all kind of shit. Going back to childhood memories I recalled the day my uncles came from South Jersey to pick up my mom and her three children. My biological dad was not a respectable man. I wanted to be better than him. I wanted to be a respectable family man. I wanted to be there for my family. My two beautiful daughters, Jessie and Julie who I love more than anything in my life. I have to be there for them.

Will I see them again? Jessica was the one that didn't talk to me. But I was determined to fix that if I can get out of this mess that I am in. ok time to fight again. I had to hold on to this pole with one hand while also holding my foot out of the water because of the sharks. Mind you I also had to hold this fucking vest that didn't fit me. I became one with this pole. My life saver, for the moment.

At that moment the bay was clam. I was thinking about my family because there was a party at my sister Nellie's house for her sister-in-law. It made me think of a tall Coors Light beer. WOW! I wish I had one now. I had to keep myself happy because I wasn't giving up. Here comes the water, starting its shit again. I see nothing in the horizon, just the dark clouds that are rolling in.

Then there was a rage from the bay. The water was really got mad cause these waves were huge. They rocked the shit out of me. I got toss around the bay from these series of waves. I hold my breath, got toss around then felt air on my skin, took another breath and waves crashing on me again. I got confused which end was up at one point. I can't tell u guys what to believe. How much longer can I really do this? What lessons do I need to

33

learn? Things happen to people and I guess it is to test their faith. On October 15 2005 my faith was tested. I felt my faith slipping from me.

The pole I was hanging on to disappear when this wave hit me so hard it knocked me off this pole. As magically as it appears hours ago, it magically disappears. I was alone. I was afraid. This is it.

I lost my pole. I lost my faith. My children lost their father. No marrying Evelyn. No more second chances.

Chapter 11

I look at the sun as it appeared it was getting ready to go to sleep and I thought it was about 5-6 p.m. I keep my body under the water but kept my eyes and nose above the waves. My body was under the water was form into a ball. I had to keep my body heat. I would move my arms so that way I could stay awake. I am starting to get a tired again. My feet have been treading water for about 6 hours. I started to fall asleep on top of the water. My eyes were heavy from the exhaustion. My body was abused from Mother Nature and her fury. I hit myself again to stay awake. Damn what a day. Then I see this red light; it was like in the distance. I thought how nice it would be if it was for me. I am tired. I want to go to asleep and not feel the pain of this terror any longer. I was tired. I hope my family knew how long I tried to live for them. I hope they remember me dearly.

Wait a minute! Am I dreaming this? Na this shit isn't happening. But the light is getting brighter and closer. I hear something. An engine. It was a boat! It is a coast guard boat. Oh God! You cannot be that cruel. Please do not tease me any longer. The red light was getting bigger and closer as the engine was getting louder. It was moving faster towards me. Oh God! They see me. I seen the top of a boat and it was getting closer. I saw men on the boat with binoculars. I started to wake up from this nightmare. Is this really happening? Am I going to live? All the sudden here comes this fucking boat. I was trying to walk on water. I woke the fuck up fast. Second chances are alive. I am alive!

The vessel came around me. A few coast guards pulled me up onto the boat. I hit my leg and I remember it should have hurt but I only remember being tossed up in the air into the boat. This vessel was huge. I remember that moment, I will never forget that.

A coast guard was asking me if there was anyone with me. I couldn't talk. Where is my voice? I was in shock and I guess from some form of hyperthermia had settling in. They kept asking is there anyone else. It felt they were screaming at me. I must have looked real bad. But I was starting to feel alive. Oh God! I was alive.

I showed them two fingers. They were asking me, two more guys. All I could do is nod my head. This one Coast guard came up to my face and looked me straight in the eyes. Where are they? I had to gather my thoughts because I had to remember which way they took off. My brothers. I had to help them find my brothers. I heard myself say they headed towards the top of the frames of the houses. So I point towards the top of the houses.

Then they put me in the haul of the boat. There were 4 guys warming me up with blankets. I mean they were going to work. They were rubbing all over me to get my blood flowing for heat. I started laughing because I was so happy to be rescued and alive. The guys on the boat ask me, why you are laughing? This one guy gave me his coast guard jacket because I was naked. So I asked them if they ever watch the Jerry Seinfeld show. They said to me, what are you talking about? So I start laughing and I remember the show when George was in the pool and his penis got shrinkage and Jerry's girlfriend walks in on George when he was naked. And they started laughing. Since I was in the water for such a long time, I had shrinkage and my 'boy' needed heat so the jacket that the guy gave me I used it to warm up my 'boy'. And then he told me to keep the jacket. That's how I have my jacket.

Justo with his Coast Guard jacket on with grandson Derek

Chapter 12

I am getting warm and I start crying because I got rescued. But I don't know what has happen with Keith and Johnny boy. Are they alive? Can the coast guards get to them in time? The boat was racing on top of the same waves they were trying to take me out. All of a sudden one of the coast guards came up to me and is telling me they found my two brothers. I couldn't believe what he just said to me. I saved their lives. At that moment I realize what happen to us. It fucking hit me. I was crying as if I was a newborn baby coming into life. I was so happy. I was so tired. But I was alive.

I was thinking about how Johnnyboy and his wife lost their triplets a few years back. They were our angels. One for each of us. Our own personal angel. We were against all odds. And they saved our lives. Angels are around us and thank the heavens we had ours.

Here comes this helicopter and it is over the boat. It's like shit you see on television and I am about to be hauled up there. Did I mention how I am scared of heights? So they hover over the boat and lower this small wire basket and I have to get into it. That was wild. I am on a boat then I get pulled up into a helicopter butt naked. I lost count how many experiences and challenges I had that day. I wanted to go home.

As soon I get pulled into the chopper the first person I seen was Johnny boy. He was crying. And telling me that he was sorry, he was so sorry. As I get into the chopper I see Keith. I lost it there. I couldn't stop hugging him. I was so happy to see my brothers. Here was a man who saved my life and I had a chance to save them. One of the crewmen offers Keith a lollipop. I grab that dam lollipop and with one bit, it was gone. Keith and I huddle for warmth. It was Johnnyboy's angels that saved us.

Chapter 13

We were in the chopper in route to the hospital. When we got to land, I bent down and kissed the ground. Yep, I sure did. I am on solid ground. We are alive from an ordeal that happens to me today. October 15th, 2005. I became emotional again. They got us to the ambulance to take us to the hospital. Keith and I were riding together. I was glad he was there. I took notice how hungry I was. I needed my family. Once the ER nurses and doctors examine me, I tried to get a hold of my family but I couldn't remember Nellie's number so I left a message on my home phone. Where was Evelyn? I was tired as I laid in the hospital stretcher. We were in different ER rooms. Jackie, Johnny boy's sister, came into my room. She was holding my hand and I wanted to know how her brother was doing. She told me he was okay but was dehydrated. She and I started to talk about the ordeal. She was so very upset. She left as the nurse came back in. I took notice Keith was not in his bed. He was hopping around with nervous energy. Keith's mom got there and she was crazed over the fact her son and his friends almost lost their lives that day. I had to call Evelyn again.

I do not recall speaking to Evelyn and telling her where I was at that moment. I gave her a brief recap of why I was at the hospital and what took place that day. She is asking too many questions. I cannot answer them now. I choose my words carefully as I am tired and don't want to get her or I upset. I just wanted to go home. I was tired. I was angry. But I could hear the fear in her voice. She sensed something was wrong. My heart hurt that she was hurting. I do love this woman. She is calling the family and she will be here soon. I just wanted to go home.

Evelyn called my sister Nellie's house right after I called her. I do not know what she said to them but it must have been brief without too much information. Maybe it is because I did not give her too much information. I heard my sister Marisol threw up from the news and my mom was stunned and wasn't able to speak. My brother in law Abe picked up Evelyn and dropped her off at Nellie's house and that is where they took off to where I was. My brother in law, Tom, drove them to me. They came alone since these two were driven with emotion to see me, hold me, and love me for many more years to come. I knew nothing was going to get in their way to bring me home. They were coming for me and I was going home.

Evelyn and my sister Nellie arrived and ran into my ER room as they verbally told the security guard they had to see me and will see me now. I cried again as emotion hit me when they stormed into my area where I was. They were standing on each side of me as I laid in the bed. We were crying happy tears to see each other. Evelyn was very upset how red I looked in my physical appearance. I must have look badly if she made a comment about my skin color. They were kissing all over me. It felt so good to feel the woman I loved in my arms. I was in her loving arms. She never held me so tight before tonight. She was scared and my sister Nell was rattling off about how the family was extremely worried. I felt safe. But I was angry. Nellie, my own flesh and blood and there's Evelyn, with her brown eyes, looking at me as if for the first time ever. They will never know how much I thought of them earlier today. My thoughts went to my daughters and how I need to see them now too!

I was released that evening and Tom took us home. He knew how to cheer me up! He brought a few beers for me in the car. Yep! I drank them in the car. My feelings were getting out of control. I was trying to console my own self. I walked into my sister's house and my parents were there. I was so happy to see them. We hugged but words escape us. It was hard to find the words. The physical hugs were great and welcomed but I was tired. I was alive. I was angry. My mom must have been dealing with her fears of possibly losing a son. We all had our demons to deal with at that moment. I just did not know for how long they were going to haunt all of us in different ways.

When we got to our own home Nellie and Tom did not want to leave me that evening. I wanted to be alone. Evelyn was running around the house trying to get my pj's. She was trying to get me to eat. She was trying to do it all. I did not want it all. I just wanted to be alone. I have unfinished private thoughts. But dam! It was good to see her. She will make a good wife. She will take care of me forever.

She wanted me to come to bed with her. As tired as I was, I could not go to bed at that moment. I needed to be alone. She was upset but trying not to show it. She didn't know how to fix the problem. It wasn't hers to fix. I had to figure this all out. I was tired. I lay on the sofa while the TV was watching me. I was so lost in thoughts. My brain would not shut off. My body aches. I was still cold. I saw the coast guard jacket. I needed it to make me feel comfortable. It became my clutch. I wore it as I finally fell asleep.

Sleep was tough. I made it upstairs finally and lay down next to her. I could not feel close to her. I felt I wanted to be alone but I also felt I needed to be in bed next to the woman I love. I had bad leg cramps that evening. I could not lay still. My brain would not stop re-acting today's event. I wanted Evelyn to be awake but I knew she had to be at work in the morning. What day was it anyway? I knew she was awake too lost in her own thoughts. We just laid there in total silence. Back to back. Motionless.

Chapter 14

I awoke in the morning and called Johnny boy. Dam no answer. I was wondering if he was still at the hospital. I smelled that Evelyn was cooking something. I did not have an appetite. The door bell rang again. It was Keith! I was as happy to see him as I did in the chopper the day before. My brother, Finally, someone who could relate the ordeal we had together. Evelyn cooked for us as Keith told his side of the story. There were parts I did not know. It brought me back to yesterday. Evelyn's face was priceless. Her expression of the emotion she was feeling while Keith was talking told it all. She loved me. She loved Keith. She just loved. I reached out to her hand as her eyes were filled with tears. Then she just jump to her feet and ran upstairs. Keith knew what I knew. She felt guilty. It wasn't her fault. It was an accident. Keith and I went out back to play cards. How can today be like any other day when we played cards? It was different. It was all different. We were trying to function as if nothing happen. Keith was eating again what Evelyn cooked. How could he eat? I had no appetite.

My baby girl, Julie came by with a ton of balloons that next day. My youngest daughter was here. Evelyn told me she was here and wanted me to open the door. I went to answer the door to let her in but how painful it was to walk. My muscles were throbbing. I was still tired. She was there and her face told me she was crying from the news. We cried in each other's arms as she walked in the house. She has brought balloons to cheer me up. It was good to see her. I was very happy she came to see me. We stood in the doorway holding each other. A daddy's love for their daughters is priceless. A daughter's love for their daddy is also priceless.

Julie had so many questions firing at me about what happen the day before. I wanted to tell her but an edit version. I was trying to piece the story and the why it had happen to us three that day. Of course, Evelyn wanted to feed us. But I just could not eat. I picked at my food. They were talking about the accident as if they were there. It was unfair they tried to explain how I was feeling. I was getting angry at the women I loved. How can they tell me or fill in the blanks. Sometimes you cannot fill in the blanks when there aren't words to convey the anger and the feelings of why me.

Julie stayed most of the day not leaving my side. She did not bring my grandson. She was protecting him from our pain. He was too young to understand. My JuJu, my first grandson Derek. His love brought me home.

People were coming by to visit. Evelyn's family came down from Philly. Mom, Chrissy and Eric were scared of what was told to them. I do not recall them breathing as Evelyn help me tell MY story. They were all concern and their love and well wishes were kind but I was tired of telling the story. I was tired. I wanted to lay down to be alone. I knew Evelyn will take care of the house when I lay down. My thoughts were rambling and not making sense. People were talking to me but it sounded as if their voices were in a distance.

Keith stayed the entire day and evening. It was hard to say good night to each other as we found comfort in each other's company. Evelyn must have cooked all day and night. I wonder if there was any food left in the house. It was nice people came to see me. I hope they knew I was appreciative of their love and concern. But I was thinking, where was Jessie? I had hoped she had come by to see me by now. I hope she knew how much I loved her. I knew one thing. I was given another chance to make things right. I had to make this happen for her and I to be father and daughter again. Why else did I live through that terror?

Julie would not leave my side that day or any other day before. Her and Evelyn stayed focus on me. Julie should be with her son but we knew he was okay. We needed this time for us. My baby daughter was my rock. It really should be the other way around. I needed to know she was going to be okay. Keith, Julie and family from Philly finally left that evening but not without a ton of I love you and hugs. We had got word that Johnny finally was released from the hospital. He will be alright. If he was feeling like me, he too wonder how long it will take to get back to life and what we use to called normal. I knew it will be with me for the remaining of my natural life. It has changed me. It placed me on a new course of prospective and life's journey. That thought was as scary as the boating accident. It has been a rebirth to correct past mistakes and trying to figure out why it had all happens. But I knew why it happens. I needed to face Jessy. I needed to make things right. She was the child and I the parent. She had to know I am not that person of the past. I need her to understand that! I need her to give me a chance to explain. It was my mistake to allow so much hurt to build up. I needed to find the courage as I did to fight for my life. Why did it seem so much more difficult than what I went through yesterday? I will make it my life mission tomorrow to see her. It had to be tomorrow.

Chapter 15

Tomorrow came and it started off the same as the day before. Evelyn was cooking and I was wondering why she wasn't at work. Am I confused about the day again? Has time just melted into one large day/night that time had no real meaning at the moment? She was not willing to leave me alone at this time. I was pleased she was here but angry she was here. I walked downstairs and I hear Evelyn speaking to my employer. She was telling him an edit version of the accident and why I won't be in for the week. I was glad she told him as I did not have the strength to tell the story again to another person. I smile at her and she understood I approve what she was doing. I went into my bathroom to avoid her questions and concerns. I wasn't upset with her but I needed more time for my thoughts. My brain just did not stop thinking. Some of the thoughts are too weird to place on this paper. I did not want to scare anyone before I can figure it out myself first.

Evelyn offer food and I tried to eat something so she wouldn't get upset. I watch her walk around and do things as she normally would do. But I just could not understand why she was normal when things just weren't normal anymore. My head was screaming with words but my body was feeling the pain of treading water. I would cough and small amounts of water try to escape my lungs. I was tired of the salty taste in my mouth, my nose just everywhere. The day started out slow until a knock was at the door. We both looked out the window and saw this beautiful angel at our doorstep. My eyes were filled with joy and I lost thought about Saturday. Do I open the door or do I let Evelyn? I guess I took so long to make a choice that Evelyn walked to the door smiling as a Christmas gift was about to be open. She opens the door and said hello to Jessy and Josh. I saw a true angel at my door. Time had stood still. I was on my feet aching to hold Jessy. She was chatting with Evelyn as I waited for Jessy to turn and see me. In that moment of time, nothing hurt, nothing matter. One of the reasons why I lived was at my door. It made sense at that very moment. Jessy walked into the house and I can see her eyes were scanning the room. She is as nervous as me. As the clouds would part to let the sun shine thru, Jessy looked at me. The day of her birth raced in my thought. She was as beautiful as that day. There stood before me was my baby girl. My heart, my daughter, my reason to live for this moment. I reached my arms out to her. We collapse into each other's arms. Tears drench us as I held her as tight as I did that dam pole in the water. I was not going to let go ever again! I realized she was holding me as tight. I was happy. I held her face and wanted to look into her eyes. Her eyes were red and swollen and her eyes were closed. She opens them and spoke the word I ached to hear, Dad. We stood there holding each other as to say our sorry's without using words in that moment. We were both proud people by culture but to see us, we looked like two crybabies.

Evelyn's voice brought me back to reality. She invited Josh in and asked if they were hungry. This woman is a cooking machine! But I was glad Jessy declined politely as her and I needed to be alone. We went out back to talk. I needed to tell Jessy my story. How she was in my thoughts. How my love for my child kept me alive.

Jessy's eyes were fixed on me while I was telling the story. She cried at parts that everyone cried but her cries were out of guilt for not talking to me for such a long time. She thought she had lost me. I could tell in her eyes she thought I was gone for a moment in time. I wanted her to know it did not matter. It was not her fault. Things happen for a reason. It was an accident. Or was it?

Jessy was here now and that is all that matter. She was eager to make up for lost time. But it truly felt that time was never lost.

My daughter is a beautiful young woman. WOW. How did I get so lucky? Man I make beautiful daughters. She looked like her mother but she had my fire. She had to tell me how she found out about the accident. She was upset that no one told her. I felt bad that she felt left out. I felt bad she felt people were not telling her because of her past actions towards me. Fuck what people think! This is my daughter and I wanted her to know only one thing. I WILL never let time come between us ever again.

We finally went in the house and I was hungry. I asked for a plate of food and Evelyn smiled. She was happy for Jessy and I. She knew faith has its reason. She had a look of calm. She is good for me. Jessy's love for me is as solid as an oak tree but as spirited as a jazz band from New Orleans.

Jessy introduced her friend Josh and we chatted for hours about the concert they attended that past weekend. She was telling me about school. She was trying to fill in the gaps of lost time. It made her feel better. I was already feeling better. I was happy to know she was enjoying life. I was even happier to know I am now a very big part of her life again. She kept smiling at me. She sat next to me on the sofa. We held hands. She was at peace. Her heart was flowing with joy. My heart was pounding. I went back to days of teaching her how to swing a baseball bat. I remember why she has two middle names. Her first birthday, her first day at school, and the days I would sign her out of school to go hang out for no reason. And to think, I almost missed this moment. I heard myself thanking God for giving me a second chance. I promise God to never forget this moment. I thank him for the second chance. I will be there and cheeriest every moment from today. My daughters: Jessica Marie Echo Lopez and with Julie Marisa Lopez.

A week or so later I return to work. I was still in physical pain and my mind was still torturing me of my experience. I was home with Evelyn and the girls and I were in constant communication. We were making plans to enjoy life's pleasures but I had the feeling of no one understood how the day in the water haunt my every waking moment. I was still feeling angry. Just did not understand why I felt angry at everything.

The holidays were quickly approaching. I had to do something before Thanksgiving. Evelyn's birthday was on Veteran Day and I had a surprise. I had to fulfill my promise to ask her to marry me. The family gathers at my brother's Angel house with all of my closest friends. Evelyn was not suspicious as it was normal to have huge birthday parties for family members. As we were getting ready to sing happy birthday I went into a speech. As I was talking, I walked over to her and got on a bent knee. I flashed back to when I told Johnnyboy that day on the boat what my plans were. I felt anxious as I was thinking of that day at this moment. I was able to get through it but as people was congratulating her and me, I was lost on that day about a month ago. Will I ever escape the torture of that day?

Work was getting more complex. Being a driver for an irrigation company I was on the road all day long. My temper was getting short and I found myself not enjoying driving. I had a great job pretty much allowed to do my own thing as long as I was on time. Driving started to become a chore. I never took notice how crazy people were on the road. I was getting road rage on the job.

The holidays were good as we were all together. Everyone was happy. It felt good to see everyone happy. My sister and brothers kept hugging me as to make up for lost time or the thought I could have been dead. Dead. The word was not in my vocabulary before the accident. I was in a haze and was afraid to share it with them. Mom kept walking around me staring at me and trying to read my thoughts. She knew something was off. But I only smiled and moved to another place to join in the idle talks. Keith became my clutch who I could only tell my deepest feelings. I felt things were getting out of control. It was very difficult for me as I live life to the fullest. I was the guy who made the parties. It was my life's mission to keep people laughing. I was not laughing inside. I had that question over my head of…….why me? Why us that day in October. I was getting angry trying to understand why it had to happen.

Chapter 16

We got married on June 3rd, 2006. It was a huge wedding and we had a blast. Everyone was happy for us and I enjoyed every moment. Evelyn looks beautiful as I had dreamt she would and I looked pretty darn good too! We were happy and October's event was starting to make sense. It was for this day to happen and we were in real time making our dream happen. The girls were in the wedding and they were not little girls anymore. They were beautiful, strong, independent women. They party like tomorrow was not going to be. I was happy their mother was there with her husband. We are family no matter that a divorce is between us. My step-son, Eric was there sharing in the family joy. He and his mom had a special danced and they looked like they were on cloud 9. Eric became more excepting of me and this meant the world to me and my new wife. We were all blending as one family. My new mother in law had a heart attack that Christmas after the accident. We had a very trying few months as a couple but it seemed to all work itself out. My mother in law was on the dance floor and she and I danced in life's special moment. I had hope. We believe in faith. Today was about Evelyn and I and the promise I made in front of Johnnyboy that prior October. Keith and Johnnyboy were in the wedding too. I was over joyous that they were there on solid ground with me, for us. Family came as far as Scotland, St. Louis and Washington D.C. to share in our joy. I felt in their minds they thought that if things went bad in October that today would have not happen. But we all got our party on that evening. Keith made a speech and in the middle of his speech, the music of the titanic started too played. It caught me off guard but everyone laugh. I guess through fear of what could have been is funny now. It was a tension release at that moment and a huge reality check what could have been. It was a day to remember. I thought I had a moment to escape the memory but many were making their toast for us that reflected that day in October. I guess it is a part of me. It swirls around me like my own mini private tornado. It is time to cut the cake. It was a good day. I have to hold it together. But my nightmares still haunted me. I lay awake many nights re-living that moment. It was a reminder that I had second chances. It is time to throw the garter. Evelyn's brown eyes are sparkling extra special this evening.

Many Months after my experience I developed an inability to work as my new wife would say. Well, let's just say I could not handle to be around people. My friends and family were living as I was getting angry at them. For what? I could not control the anger. I wanted to talk about it daily but Evelyn told me one day, to get over it. Why did she say that? That was a fight I never forgot. It was our first real battle. I lashed out to her. I said things that should have not been spoken but I was angry. She was upset. She walked away from me and went upstairs and that was the last thing I needed. I was alone again. Just like in the water. Stranded alone. Wild waves were in my head. I had to leave. This time, my legs were able to get me going. I stormed out the house. I had to be with anyone. I just could not stay alone.

I came home late that evening from driving. I could smell she was in the kitchen. There she goes Again being normal. Why can't people understand? Life was not normal anymore. Do I really need to engrave it on my forehead?

I ended up losing my job. I had no interest. I was tired of people and their ability to only be normal. Surprisingly Evelyn told me to give it up. She was tired of hearing me bitching about people. Evelyn came home one day and she sat me down. Here we go. We just got married and she was going to give me a lecture. I heard what she had to say and I was happy that she loved me. She suggested to me to see a therapist. She felt it would help as she was as frustrated as I. She did not want fight with me. Divorce was not an option. I felt bad I was putting her through this. But she wanted to get back to normal. There was no more normal.

I saw a few therapists. Some did not get me at all, but this one therapist only wanted to give me drugs to forget. There was this one drug they gave me called Zoloft that Evelyn ended up throwing in the trash. She gave me one pill and when she came home that evening, I was in the same position as she left that moment. She found me drooling on myself and I do not recall anything about those hours she was at work. She was yelling in the house threaten to cause harm to anyone who tried to treat me with drugs. I never knew she can get so upset! But I like going to the therapist but they wanted me to admit myself into a program. Evelyn hit the roof on that issue. She was very eager to help me, but we had to find a balance right for us. It wasn't about me anymore. She was still blaming herself somehow. I resented that she felt that way. She doesn't have to be mad. She just has to love me and take care of us. Keep us on track. She can't lose it now!

Keith wasn't around after the wedding and months to follow. He went to work for his brother up north and I missed his company. We lost contact with each other. I really felt I lost a lot that day in the water. I was just starting to realize how much. He was there and I didn't have to fill in any blanks when he was around. He knew how I felt as I knew how he was feeling. But do I really know the demons we face with life's changing moments? We have to find what works best for us as individuals and try to blend it in our lives.

Last Chapter........Not!

It has been ten years now since the accident. We have three grandsons now. Julie gave us our second grandson name Jasaias and he is like her. Full of fire. Evelyn says he is like me and she might be right. He is full of life and enjoys being around people. Julie is due any day now with her third child but it is a girl. My very own little Julie, a baby girl. How good life has been from that one horrible moment that haunts me from my past. Jessy has a wonderful son named Donny the 3rd who I call D3 for a nickname. All my grandchildren will have nicknames for them. I am a pop-pop Justo and that is what we do! The girls are women now and are happy. They are somebody's mommy and this carries a lot of responsibilities. I can only guide them in their journey but I wish them nothing less than the very best. They have everything that is important for them. They have a family of their very own and many people who love them endlessly. Life is great after 9 years of marriage. Evie and I are happy and we brought our first home a few years ago. Everything about this house is for the kids. We have a cat and three dogs. One of Dogs whom I call baby Justo because I tease the girls since none of their sons is named after me. LOL. Evelyn and I do not have our own biological children but she loves the girls and grandchildren as if they were her very own. She is here forever. She has made a house into a home where I can be safe and be me. She lets me do crazy decorating ideas in the house but somehow they get turned around and corrected by her. She says the only steps in our home are the ones that let us inside of the house. But I am happy my girls learned one thing from me. Do you. The fuck with what people think. Do you!! I am a family man now. The head of a growing family. They look at me for wisdom and laughter. Thank God laughter is still a large part of my life. Eric called me dad somewhere after the wedding. It was nice to have a son I could be a part of his life. He and the girls were like sisters and brother. We felt and look like a family to the world. But Eric's death is tough on us all. I lived to see my wife in so much immense pain but I have to be there for Evelyn as she has been for me. She is such a strong woman to carry such a burden for the remainder of her life. My burden is for the rest of my life too. Our burdens together keep us close.

Evelyn is a manager at the hospital and keeps taken care of things and people. The entire burden this woman carries and she is always thinking of others. Maybe that is why we found each other 14 years ago. So I have someone to take care of me and her needing to take care of someone. I wonder what she would do without the girls and grandchildren now that Eric is in heaven. How does she manage her feelings? She must know something I have not yet to learn. I try to manage my feelings but it will always be with me. I am sure her only son's death is with her too. But we talk about those feelings but I am willing to bet she doesn't tell me everything she is feeling as I do not tell her. We understand each other and again, give each other the space that is needed to keep our sanity. I have my good days and bad but now people around me give me my space without making comments. They allow me to be me. It is accepted.

Johnny boy has done many projects on the house for us. We have a bond. It is an unspeakable grip. He has a daughter and he and Jennifer are happy. We don't talk about that dreaded October in fear that today might be a dream and not a reality.

Keith and I have renewed our friendship. But the truth is it was never lost. He got married two summers ago as he tells me he found his own Evelyn. Her name is Courtney and she is perfect for my brother. I am so happy for him. I am glad we went to their grand wedding. I am happy that he asked me to be in the wedding. I made sure his day was as special as mine was. Full of love, good memories for us all to share.

The cooler of fish we caught before the sea tossed us around was the trigger that had these fishermen call for help. These guys were out there fishing that day too and when they saw a cooler of fish floating in the bay, they called over the radio to report their findings. That was when the coast guard sent out a chopper. I met them a few years ago and we had a fish story to tell. It felt great to tell them how appreciative and glad I was that they were there. Angels do walk with us in many different areas in our lives.

But I still have nightmares that I deal with when they come. I know now, I have to fight thru them as I did on October 15th, 2005.

My uncle (tio) Marcel Ramos died in the same waters as few years after the boating accident. Three friends spent the day after Stripers and the boat turned over and my uncle died in the waters that tried to take me. Were those waters trying to grab my attention? They wanted me to remember just how powerful water is in the universe. It was hard to call mom. First it was me then her brother in the same waters. We never really discuss her thoughts but I felt fear was close to her concerns.

I lived through that day in October 2005 to come to this moment. It is one huge circle of life. I am 52 yrs old now and I realized life is full of experiences. Some are good and others are, let's just say, things we deal with in our own way. I just hope people remember the good and they surround themselves with people who accept and love them as my family/friends have done for me.

In writing my adventurous life of my past ten years, as I have relived a moment that is with me every day. Through love and patience of others, I am able to write. Evelyn is a huge part in this story. There were nights I could not write and she would jump in to help me get this out on paper. I had nightmares often and kept to myself in my space. We had augments but we found how to balance it all to make it work. I am happy now. I have other journeys to walk and fortunate to be alive. Thank you God for second chances. I now understand and I am at peace.

I now suffer from; Post traumatic Stress Disorder. P.T.S.D for short. It's a disorder that takes you back to things that happen to you while the bad things that happen in your life or should I say traumatic events in your life. I deal with it every day and my own way. I have found that writing poems really help me out a lot. I feel as though I can help others with these poems and now I really have a following of friends and family that expect a poem every day. I don't write on the weekends it's my family time on the weekends. That's family time. This year makes ten wonderful years that the good Lord has let me live. I have taken advantage of these ten years and fulfill a lot in my life.

Justo and family members on Mother's Day

My family and friends love the loving and caring Man that I have become. I guess what I went through has changed me for the better. When Evelyn and I lost our son Eric back in January 12th, 2014, it was really hard to handle because even though he was my step son, but he was my Son.

Because he choose to call me Dad, I *dedicate* this book to the memory of my only Son, Eric A. Cruz. "Son, you are deeply missed, but we will never ever forget you and your essence."

We miss you Eric…. Until later, I hope I can see you at the Pearly White Gates

~~Justo Lopez Jr…..

"Motivation"

How can you break free from the chains that bind you?
Is it lack of motivation that holds you back from what you do?
I was motivated to stay alive………..
I was lost in the ocean and that ain't no jive,
Three people became brothers on that fateful day,
Three men are bonded in a very special way,
For lost we all are sometimes,
I am just glad that it wasn't my time.
I wrote this book to set me free,
To let me become the Man I was meant to be,
Live life til the very end,
I do it every day, my friends.

~~Justo Lopez Jr.

Justo and Eric at our 80's party a few years ago we hosted. We had a blast that evening. Eric and one of his bear hugs.

Julie, Jessy, Derek and Eric (Julie is carrying Jasaias)

Justo and Evelyn

Justo, Jessy and D3, Three generations

Justo Lopez Jr.

Jessy, Justo, Eric, Donny Jr., grandson D3

Justo, Evelyn, and Julie

The head of the family

I went to my daughter Jessy and asked her to write in her own words how she felt the day she heard I was in the boating accident. Here is her reaction.

(Jessica M.E. Lopez – Justo's oldest daughter)

"I remember waking up from a deep sleep and wanting to go downstairs to get something to eat. I made myself some breakfast and began eating when my grandmother Mima walked in the door. The first words out of her mouth were "como estas tu Papa?" Almost immediately, my mother and I both looked at one another like "why is she asking that question?" I responded and said that I didn't know, but assumed that he was doing well. See, I chose not to speak to my dad after my parents were divorce for a very long time and our relationship deteriorated as a result. Therefore, I was so confused as to why my grandmother was asking me a question like that considering how she knew I didn't speak to my father. I never asked my grandmother why she wanted to know how my father was doing and went upstairs to get a shower.

After I got out of the shower, I went downstairs to talk to my mom. When I walked into the kitchen, she told me to sit down because she had something to tell me. Immediately, I could feel my heart pumping faster and faster imaging the worst. However, everything that I imagined at that very moment was not what she was about to tell me! She said to me "your dad was in a boating accident and they don't know if he is going to make it!" I felt paralyzed at that moment! I wanted to speak, but nothing would come out. I wanted to cry, but no tears flooded my eyes. I wanted to escape, but could not run. My mother kept speaking, but I was trying to come to grips with the fact that my father may not make it. I felt like I was in a movie and the only sound that you could hear was that of my heart beat!

I went upstairs to my room because I wanted to be by myself. I sat on my bed with my hands holding my head and thought about all the good times that I had with my father. I had flash backs of his boisterous voice and dominating personality. I could hear his voice in my head and I felt in my heart that there was no way that it was his time. That whatever occurred in this "boating accident" would not take my father's physical spirit. As I was holding my head, I kept saying to myself there is no way that my dad could die not knowing that I loved him and I wasn't upset with him anymore. Or that I knew that he tried to be in my life but that I just pushed him away out of anger. I felt like a complete ass and thought that my dad may give up in his fight to live because he knew our relationship deteriorated. Well the truth is, all the years that I hated my father, I really loved him! I never stopped loving him, but I would never show it or let him know it! I wanted my father to realize the potential he had at becoming a great father. The potential he had at being a wonderful husband. I wanted my Dad to get healthy and live for his two children.

I hadn't thought about how I felt about my father in a while and I was overwhelmed with emotion that I just broke down. I felt like, how could I cry for my father when I treated him as if I disowned him? How could I go visit him in the hospital where he was in, when hate once filled my heart for him? I had no right to even though I was his daughter by law and by blood. I mean, before this accident, I never treated him with the respect that a daughter should have for their father. It was my sister Julie who maintained her relationship with him and not me. Therefore, she had every right to feel more pain than I did. She had every right to feel broken and like a piece of her heart was breaking from the horrible news. I felt as if my family would be the first to point out that I hated my dad so what am I doing crying over him. I mean, my family never called me in the first place to tell me that my dad was in an accident. If my grandmother Mima didn't go to church that Sunday Morning, she would have never heard my grandmother Edith ask the church members to please pray for her son because he was involved in a horrible accident. Moreover, she would have never come over to my mother's house to ask "Como estas tu Papa" and I would have not known that my father was involved in an accident that would essentially change his whole life and mine!

Deep down inside, I wanted to go see my dad that Sunday morning when my mother told me about his boating accident, but I didn't. I didn't go see him right away because I thought to myself, why would he open the door to someone who treated him so horribly? And it was my friend Angel who said to me, "Jess, you know your dad always loved you no matter how hard you pushed him away. So, what makes you think at his most vulnerable moment, that he is going to turn your back to you?" He was absolutely right. My dad was like a green head fly that would come back after the first, second, and third swat of the hand. In fact, he probably would have died trying to amend our relationship before he ever gave up on me. So I decided to go see my dad at his apartment and let go of this enormous elephant that I had been carrying around for years on my back!

I went over with one of my friends Josh to visit my dad. As soon as he opened the door and I saw his face we embraced and it felt like time stood still. Like, I didn't need to say out loud to him that I was sorry because he could feel it through my hug. I hadn't hugged my father like that in years and it felt good! We cried and went out back to talk some more and I was able to release all of my emotions that I had buried inside of me for years. I listened to him tell me everything that happened and it was probably the hardest thing I've ever had to listen to. My dad is a strong, dominate, and fighter of a person. To hear him get choked up and actually see tears coming out of his eyes, literally broke me down. There was a moment where he was describing to me how he was floating in the water and decided that he had "given up." He had no more fight in him. Then he said he started to think about how he needed to fix our relationship and get me back in his life. At that moment, I had this weird thought. I thought that God has a plan for everyone and things happen for a reason. Meaning, in my mind, there was a reason that God wanted me to be born to Justo Lopez and Peggy Rivera. There was a reason why God decided at the age of nine, that it was time for my parents to get a divorce. There was a reason why I chose not to speak to my father for multiple reasons. There was a reason that my father went fishing that day with two of his friends and their boat sank. My dad needed a reason to survive and I just happened to be one of those reasons. The whole time I'm listening to my father speaks his story, I couldn't help but thank God that it was him to be the one to tell me. I thanked God for allowing me the opportunity to tell my dad, I forgave him and that I loved him because if my dad had died in that boating accident, I don't think I would be the happy person that I am today! That night, we spoke our peace and that was the beginning of our newer relationship as father and daughter. I love you dad forever and thank you for NEVER giving up!! I don't know that I could have lived without you! I can't imagine life without you and don't want to!"

~~~~Jessica M.E. Lopez

Printed in the United States
By Bookmasters